Rank Songbirds

Happy Birthday to Paula

Love
[signature]

Rank Songbirds

LEON ROOKE

The Porcupine's Quill

Library and Archives Canada Cataloguing in Publication

Title: Rank songbirds / Leon Rooke.
Names: Rooke, Leon, author.
Description: Poems.
Identifiers: Canadiana (print) 20210386452 | Canadiana (ebook) 20210386479
 | ISBN 9780889844483 (softcover) | ISBN 9780889844490 (PDF)
Classification: LCC PS8585.O64 R36 2022 | DDC C811/.54—dc23

Copyright © Leon Rooke, 2022.

1 2 3 · 24 23 22

Published by The Porcupine's Quill, 68 Main Street, PO Box 160, Erin, Ontario N0B 1T0. https://porcupinesquill.ca

All rights reserved. No reproduction without prior written permission of the publisher except brief passages in reviews. Requests for photocopying or other reprographic copying must be directed to Access Copyright.

Edited by Chandra Wohleber.

Represented in Canada by Canadian Manda. Trade orders are available from University of Toronto Press.

We acknowledge the support of the Ontario Arts Council and the Canada Council for the Arts for our publishing program. The financial support of the Government of Canada is also gratefully acknowledged.

1

Come now, let's
Roll around on the floor like
We are God's scruffy minions
Let loose from paradise on a day pass or to enjoy a weekend in the country
I will hold your hand I will say sweet words into your ear
I will comb your hair after a cooling swim in the river of mirth or
Read to you a gentle story as night falls   oh
The night is enchanting is it not though
What relief when morning faithfully arrives
And with it a breakfast of sorts, hot coffee at any rate,
Make mine Cuban Mexican French Italian Greek in a pinch
Do you employ sugar, madam?   certainly not
Cream?   beg pardon, cream never   surely
I am not perceived as one of those effete creatures installed
In green garden high on a plinth
In expectation of redeeming luxury   to put it another way
How long must I live with you before you learn my name or
Is my name finally the name of all those you've professed adoration for
Through your expansive holiday with love   all
That hand-holding business which comes to nothing I
Might well say my hopes were dashed the moment I
Hooked up with you, hooked, did I say hooked,
Hooked is not the word I would utilize for what
Assailed me although it is true your lovely poodles and I
Loved you with full heart in every corner of the corridors of desire
In full expectation of the occasional expectation of merciful understanding
If rarely such was ever to be glimpsed, a man thing I suppose, whatever
Those in the higher realm of witchcraft might claim.

              Ah and yet and yet and yet again how
Effortless, how splendidly effortless giving this love was,
How intrepid we were and continue to be!
Such an overflow scoop it up with a bucket, Mother said
One should run and fetch a mop dear
Our every window misted over
By your hot breathing, how indecorous of you.
Did we raise you, poor Daddy said
To roll your heels to the first boilermaker tipping his hat?

              How impaired we surmised these unloving parents to be
Did their spirit conjoin in the dark mystery of abandoned railway
Stations to which life's engine never arrived poor Daddy Choo Choo
And plain old flatfooted Mary his crumb
Treading softly on worn pilgrim feet

            Yet still the sun so brightly blinding to our
Eyes year in year out, years, all but without end we liked to think,
God's own hot-house warriors at work and play

So come now don't dally no moping allowed today for
Here breaks the breaking news   let's
Paint the sky a modest blue
Throw in a tree or two   scatter
Grass seed about   do
I am saying God's work since
We do agree do
We not   everything
Worthwhile to be done
Has been left to us.

    ❏

2

My beloved cannot, may not, will not execute
The unworthy act   hold
Her pretty feet to the fire   set
Entire cities ablaze   prod
Her with the ironmonger's hot poker,
Withhold lemonade, shout a vigilante's heated threat
She will in no way tolerate the unworthy act though thieves waylay her,
Waters be shaken by hurricane,
Collapse of the very streets on which her feet set down.

Here, she says, hold my hand
Say me no platitudes
Lower no empty bucket
Into my well
Simultaneously don't be suckered by a girl's soft speech   flush
Of rosy cheek   flash
Of leeward limb
The bonny disposition of starlets on parade   look:
Me once a mere old-fashioned girl faint of heart, grace, and intellect   see
How pigeon-toed and halting my every step, a witless child   stirred
To tearful disarray by any shadow haunting floor or wall   an unkind word
Found the woman you are said to love   shivering
Through night's repast   Fathom me
Now chewing to the bone
These very fingernails, my ratcheting sobs   was
That only yesterday?

3

Look deeply into these eyes where you may perceive
The wealth of a voyager's dream not likely
To be confused with faltering circumstance—your failing speech,
The stuttering tongue, the hawk shift of wavering eye
Perhaps you should take this chair beside mine   sit
Contemplating your shuttered past
The mayhem of remembered days
Lunging up and down the thorny hills of lust.
No omen quakes you   Shame
Has yet to embalm you   Shaft
Those demon wraiths wasting you,
Apply love's bandage to the shiftless heart
This minute pooling debris about your feet,
How quaint you look, how doleful you are,
I am possibly moved to feel a droplet of sympathy
For you there waylaid along the path of fallen prince.
Do I see some glimmer of remorse, some slippage in the brain
No I thought not   even so
And how heroic I am   ever
The fool, listen closely my darling knave
For full cure simply   observe
These hips twisting through our tall grass
Sown only yesterday, the sky I waked early to freshen
With new paint, a rudimentary eggshell blue I believe it is,
You'll see there our tree already bearing fruit
I do wonder what kind, so tasty I am sure
The very thought elevates me   behold
The lovely apparition now undressing you   resign
Yourself to this siege of kisses falling free as honey
Pouring from a high shelf
May I suggest you stroke a warm shoulder
Unburden your leaded hands by touch of my neck
Unsheathe a breast   slowly now
First one, then   why yes
Why not both   of course
Your lips may venture there

What a brave hoodlum you are
Though take a moment to   gander
Studiously upon these long legs
Experience teaches me the more expansive gaze   always
Always works
Thus and so thus and so
Such fine mettle you are in today
Here within our new tall grass
The fruit-bearing tree put to earth a mere yesterday,
Why not shout your love with glass-blower's heat,
View me as ransacking lover miscreant
Installed fresh daily from the loom,
Have not fabled historians and saints alike concluded
After kitchen clean-up, after child-rearing, after obedience,
Timeless servitude to neglectful oligarchs
Which in the last mile most of you are   this
Above all else remains woman's work?

⊠

4

Sky-blue blouse, matching eyes,
Hand darting through golden hair:
Your beautiful wife is home:
Pinch of cayenne
Fresh basil from the porch
Chili powder
Onions chopped
Throw in those bewitched tomatoes
Unwatered in the field.
Actually it was dinner
On her mind   this
Creating the hue and cry
Following discovery of another
Dreaded pound:

'In point of rudimentary fact
My face is actively plain
Never having wish to dress it up
My hair is I suppose sufficiently thick
Though I'd be lying to claim
It ever gleamed
I stand average in height or average
For this hemisphere   posture
No better than OK, good shoulders though,
Routine breasts may be supposed,
Smidgens of chubbiness buttressing waist and hips,
Sorry to report my thighs quiver as well
Muscle vacated to foreign shore
Still it's true these lengthy legs inspire goodwill,
Many the squandered sigh
At my divinely rendered *berceuse*,
How exhausted I am by the thousand men
Swabbing their decks in anticipation
Of the arrival of my dancing feet.

I believe my smile accounts for this,
My cultured voice,
Oftentimes it's something simple like that,
Do you concur?'

5

When he was painting his infamous Mile
Of Smiling Nudes a favoured model
Was prone to nibbling from a wedge of cheese.
He liked her high on a table
'For the bone-throned sweep of you,' he said.
She sometimes arrived with a child
Both mounting the table to nibble the cheese,
The child secured inside a basket since
In pure terms he was hardly yet one
And liked crying better than cheese.
'But it's French cheese,' he might shout,
The model in relentless disavowal
Saying, 'I'll not have it I tell you
I'll not have you painting a single tear
In the frightened eyes of our love-child.'
Miles and miles of these naked women,
Critics ever asking why his fat babies
Carry naught but smiles. 'Bit redundant
You know de Kooning's the better approach,
Should have taken Modigliani's cue
Left the babies at home.'

6

What's this? You want to compete for this year's
Bad Sex award, you want me to offer guidance, inspiration,
'til you're on your feet again? What's that, you intend
Not merely to compete but to win
This year's Bad Sex award, in the endeavour
For which you hold my participation vital?
You want those sharpie judges at the Literary Review
To motorboat-swoon with pure joyous envy
At the sheer unequalled capacity of your Bad Sex prose?
Say what? What was that again? I'm to be your throbbing, whooping
Babe gone cross-eyed from sheer unadulterated pleasure! Practical practice,
You say, of the practical act
Will summon us into the winner's field?
You are confident I am up to the task?

Here, darling, hold my hand. Yes, that one. Let's begin
With the simple embrace. Timid peck of the cheek. No, no,
Put the tongue back into your mouth. Don't squirm.
Plant your feet solidly on the floor. That's good.
Or good enough. Yes, yes. What commanding presence
You possess.

7

Tonight
I'll serenade you
With kisses
Modestly dressed

8

If I were to give up beauty
First I'd have to give up you

But what if I became innocently lost
How would you find me?
Quick   take our picture   glue it
To the wall.

9

First, we set a course on the yoga thing. This ended in the negative. Next, seeking a thing we'd heard about called inner peace, we endured a bout of meditation lasting months. Deeper and deeper this meditation hurled us, until at last we were in blackest underground with seemingly no way out, a condition we found quite harrowing because during this period we were without the morning grapefruit we liked so much. We heard people working with noisy excavation tools in an apparently foolhardy attempt to reach us. Sometimes obnoxious sniffer dogs slurped our faces in willful pursuit of the abiding doubt any living mortals resided down there. Leaflets fell at our feet, offering instruction on the proper meditative practice. 'Comfortable clothing is mandatory,' someone shouted. 'Don't slouch,' added another. Picture books were dropped down. It's transcendental, stupid, you are not meant to understand it, these pictures proclaimed: DOCUMENTED EVIDENCE OF THE PATHWAY TO ETERNAL LIGHT. Days and nights flit by. Nothing. Nothing, nothing, nothing. Flitting by. What peace, what tranquillity that nothingness was. Next, to discern this most raucous sounding fit to split the ears. Car horns, bleating voices, stampeding feet. Salvation, of a kind. Finally, however unlikely, friends, lynx-eyed neighbours, fraught restaurateurs had decided they missed us, they wanted fellowship, a return to the good old days—sumptuous drinks by the fire, a delicious dinner, fine prolonged discussion of judicious issues, a laugh or two. So, in the end we admitted our ignorance, focusing never having been a strong suit. So, So, we just sat down and cried, holding each other tightly in neat compositions of love. Our convalescence this period may be called, one requiring extraordinary delicacy in speech and movement, given that

>we are not the
>flagrant
>exhibitionists
>you likely are.

10

The good wife, head of the household, now avariciously composed, is eager to astonish loutish colleagues at Massey Hall with her new divination: that magnate of higher literature, Anton P. Chekhov, before whom unbuckled women universally swooned, tirelessly depicted in his pages women as nonsensical popinjays devoid of merit. The brute had, late in life, to meet and be overcome by Lydia Mizinov and Olga Knipper, not to mention a labyrinth of 28 others, before understanding the first particle of love. Oh the broken hearts flagpole-high in number. A swine. Like you, my adored one. When I shout, of night, 'Come to bed,' you shall in future arrive instantly, this romance otherwise is curtains.

11

She has renamed herself Cassandra   Observe
How this Cassandra flits room to room shouting
Does it matter, Cassandra, as we stack the furnace with logs
In roast of marshmallows liked by no one   here
She gallops again, these words flung like kites in the alien field,
Her voice ascending as adoring Apollo calmly scopes out marshmallows
On flaming sticks. Does it matter, Cassandra, this question
Summoned again by another day's heavy news, four schoolgirls
    murdered in Alabama,
Addie Mae, 14, Cynthia, 14, Carole, 14, Carol Denise, 11,
Does it matter, Cassandra, that the congregation afoot on your lawn
Is not stirred to acceptance of your harried truth—
Vile thugs, rubes, demented racist pleasure killers
Waving made-in-America swastika caps in the sworn hope
Of pulverizing all such Cassandras, shove them through a meat grinder,
Along with the Collins girl, Addie Mae, 14, the Wesley girl, 14,
The Robertson girl, 14, the McNair child, 11 ('We are in expectation
Of gittin' two more by nightfall'). Constipated pigs, declares Cassandra,
Frenzied goat-belly bitch, hum they back, while up in the nation's capital
J. Edgar Hoover removes his suit and tie, makes himself comfortable,
Says to the assembly,
    Now shall we have tea?

12

City fathers installed two fountains on City Hall lawn, one for Us the other for Them. Unknown to us was were we us or them, having arrived from afar and fried of outlook as pertains to local affairs, but being made posture-free by the summer heat we learned the Us fountain flowed weak root beer, the other a liquid rather sharp on the tongue. A limping dark fellow shrouded in gloom approached us saying you should know you are drinking my blood, which remark rattled us a bit as we looked him over most particularly. Not just mine, he said, but also my son's, my daughter's, my parents' and grandparents' and those before them in the long march, whereas your Us over there is plain old A&W root beer, sweetened somewhat to harmonize with the heavenly destiny awaiting you and which day I so solemnly pray will soon come. Excuse us, we piously inquired, are you by chance the sainted Dr. King?

At your mercy, said he.

Somehow City fathers got wind of the alien visit, a delegation arrived at our door, a visitation causing such alarm we took to our broomsticks, passing quickly into other realms, only a few of those Cityhallers taking to theirs, likely having fountains to repair. We held lofty dialogue while in flight pertaining to that degenerate fellow Sisyphus, trying so hard to get the loathsome boulder up the hill, she asking what I thought the hill in question thought about the business, the hill reminded, she argued, of the endurance required to bring itself to full maturity, the hill having considered itself in a prior age a self-made hill. The other hills looking over in wonder at the Sisyphus hill and shrinking in sheer cognition of their own ineptitude at becoming a part of history. I said to her this subject holds no interest for me, it has no connection whatever to that City Hall stuff—to which she replied

Your intellectual barriers
Have ever flummoxed me
My parents were right
I have wed a dodo
If not a dodo
Then a Judascake
I am no longer talking to you.

13

Apology accepted, we need
Trading in these broomsticks
Consult the yellow pages
Some matters can't be put off 'til next week

14

What would we do without our religions a stranger asked   We
Would not know one leg from the other   What
Use to put them to   My hair would cease its growth,
Sending ten billion beauticians in search of the soup line
Provided such line existed, which is reason enough for putting up
With this faith business, don't you think?   Don't you?
We like saying old Johnny terrorized neighbours,
died and went to hell in a hail of bullets, who knows?
I personally can't claim on a stack of whatever stack of
Persuasion thumped onto the table where he did or didn't go,
Although I certainly hold assured views on that, never mind those
Contemplative bastards telling us he was such a good friendly sort,
Liked baseball, would give you his last dime, never drowned a cat   We
Don't know if he enjoyed last rites, did he drag himself
From barbed-wire floor to be baptized one sunny day,
Or something else, we know he was often a rat at the best of times,
Somewhat akin to a jellyfish, so it's said,
I am content to let religion settle this Johnny's fate   Are you
Not with me on this?

15

Vouchsafe here
The means whereby my near-perfect body atones
While I bestow my and dare I say
Your many children onto the universal stage   some
Of these to be considered mouthy orphans if not exasperated psychopaths
As I myself may be construed as one befitting the socially
    induced mould.   Oh,
But that cannot be true. I say such in consideration
Of those personal moments when proper breathing fails me post-embrace
Of developing news: Barking Woman Walking Dog Breaks Leg.
Potato Farmer From Shenyang Avers Hourly Recitation Of
    'The Maiden's Prayer'
Saves Unwed Sister's Melon Field.
While here in these parts (I am speaking of the home front):
Mad Hyena Missing The Throat Has Thought To Run Away
    With My Mangled
Foot (following another of those debilitating miserable moments
    when devising
A dinner menu acceptable to all has again eluded me):
Pie of buckwheat groats, soup heaped with rooted vegs: a no-go.
    Eel turbot savvy *Bon Vivant*
recommends (mind the sprats, the gobies, the mollusk shells)
    but first cloak the head in savoury
chickpea batter, making sure said eel (non-electric) is pulled from nearby
    river, pond, or palace
moat and, hence, known as freshly dead.
    Or:
Simple Grade A farm-loved egg with grits and huckleberry, slime removed.
    Or this:
Young duck in dripping pan with potatoes chinked small to cut the lard.
Pickled kidney over bed of beets, for loved ones, if depraved.
Brace of smoked carp with fettered escargot over briny underleaf
Is rumoured nymph-sweet to tongue and nose, said to be a boon
To obese diners short of breath.

Slab of highland goat (Scots) flavoured within overnight soak
In broth of sumac leaves, appropriate wines and grappa hits a must.
The table candlelit, you prairie rubes.
Will today's dinner be delayed? Why, yes, isn't it so? My near-perfect feet
At perfect rest on pillowed hassock, martini glass deftly in hand.
Do not assume full rot awaits. What personality
These personalities of TV cooking shows generate,
How robustly enthusiastic they are. If they brought the same
    to democracy
World poverty, bad water in refugee camps, the migrant flow
Would be no more. New Years with no beginning, the old without end.
For me today (I am so thinking), boeuf bourguignon! But what of our
    vegetarian fold?
No help *Good Housekeeping* think to plow into *Larousse Gastronomique*.
But Godzilla nor Hercules could lift that pinch-printed book.
The *Good Eats Bible Cookbook*, ever a prize.
    Truly I tell you this very night
Before the rooster crows twice, you will deny me three times.
Adam comes home from the hunt, his beaming other says,
'Look at the nice apple pie I have made, am I not a woman
    beyond compare?'
Oh me. Our cupboard is bare, moths in the flour bag,
    scouring the ragged kinship
Pages of *Joy of Cooking* no help, admit it, Cassandra,
    your canned peaches
Ferment a poisonous brew, she's unreliable, dear poppa liked saying,
    I'm fed up
With her left-winger crap whilst I gnaw my fist to bone
Keeping the universe composed, give them
An education this is what it comes to, I'll never forgive her
The dead butterfly she placed atop my eggs benedict.

16

As for that turbot's defining ingredient,
When husbands forget your birthday,   go amuck   make
The claim that prose 'o'ertakes poetry at every falling,' that hallowed sages
Of line and word 'were not that much'
(Frost, Mr. Pound, Mr. Eliot, *all* 'confessional' poets were mentioned)   take
This down: the gristle of one sheep,
One heap of Yukon potato for crust crucial for disguise
Of hat pins buried within   laudatory
Dish special to those evenings when you've discovered
Your hoodlum husband is a prick provocateur   (you can forget
His 'I was kidding')   not (I hope)
That one of your elevated rank could ever   share
This sad experience   I believe
I can be forgiven my six-month jaunt through Merteventura,
or was that the time I took up arms with insurgents in El Salvador?

17

I am so sorry am I to report those I love, your children I mean, have fled
For safekeeping to the city zoo so far to the town's edge no way may they
Ever return. Let's admit several of these were sappy offspring hardly existing
In the first place. In fact I had other worries wetting my brain, for instance
This business of your immediate girlfriend I chanced to run into
    on the broken pavement
By a seaside emporium rich with imported Peruvian artifacts,
Me there with my Ph.D. comparing trimness of ankle, the pricey haircut,
The exquisiteness of leather on shoe and purse, what good luck, thought I,
To be smart and rich plus in childish dream the most beautiful woman
    any mortal
Ever looked upon. Whereupon, striding up from ragged stalls by the seashore,
A true paragon appeared, surely Miss Universe of each coming year.
    This woman's
Admirers stretched to the end of Xanadu, not to mention
    the transfixed or howling
Many in open doorways. Men leapfrog at sight of me, this darling said,
    you'd believe
They were jumping rope, such gazelles! What a woman, declared I to this
    laughing perfection,
You deserve him, if not both of us. How interesting, said she,
    or was about to say
When a restless wind unloaded a sea of unearthly dust upon us,
There we to reside until a kinder breeze slung us into weedy ditch,
Which in the best manner possible
                    received us.

❋

18

What I ask you, oh great traveller, means this Statement of Charges from the Odeon Hotel, Paris, France, one week's stay at 1,800 euros, and this one, by rumour a Balzac and Chateaubriand hang out, La Closerie des Lilas, 500 euros for your daily *foie gras de canard*, your grilled turbot, how can this be when you know not a syllable of French, when you have been by my side every minute of every day, why was I not with you on the gay journey, I who have words to say to this Balzac's chase of rich widows through the whole of his immature life. And here in this sheaf I see Morocco, a month-long sit-down with your pal Bowles, not to mention that strung-out pile of beat-freaks or radiant wordsmith Jane. Hell's bells, don't attempt extricating yourself, you will only dig a deeper hole, the guilt, your eyes express the bitter truth, and another thing, kindly to stop pawing at me, get yourself a dog if you're wanting love, as for me I have booked a morning flight, my shoulder bag is packed, I have serious need
    for new shoes
    steep in the heel
    that I may tower
    over everyone.

19

The new piano has an attractive personality, is mostly attentive
To our needs, and unlike the previous model pauses when
The telephone rings though it refuses to take messages
Except from those callers wanting to talk to the baby. The baby
For reasons unexplored thinks the piano's name is Archie and often
We hear the baby shouting, 'Archie shut up,' sometimes,
'Archie ate my peanuts.' Cassandra has been heard to admit
The new piano has flaws: it will only play Mozart who rouses us from bed
Each morning, summons us to bed come early evening,
Usually when we'd prefer another activity.
I list as example Mozart's piano sonata #16 (morning)
His flute concerto #1 (evening). Euphoria verges into the sublime,
The baby may say on hearing the latter. Of certain ariosi the baby
Is notably fond, he would like these sections extended or repeated,
But the new piano refuses, the new piano habitually tells him
To stop acting silly, are you a nincompoop, a drooling fool
Deposited on my doorstep? The wife and I often feel
An awful nostalgia for the old piano, which was far less judgmental, was not
Cataclysmic in mood, kept to regular hours, did not drink, liked vacuuming.
Was helpful in the kitchen. The old lady who sold us the new piano
Confesses that while under her keep it only did Bach. 'And not well,' she said.
'Getting shut of that quarrelsome bastard will add twenty years to my life.
    The red Pontiac
You see in my driveway has an utter disregard for stopped school buses,
Uses abusive language when crossing a bridge, chases barking dogs.
Are you interested?'

20

Noon did not arrive today.
We heard the clock's struggle,
Demonstrated remorse for the moaned syllables
Of cuckoo bird's earlier weathered squawk,
Sacrificed our time by wearying river walk,
Consulted authorities said to be informed,
Were told the flaw was temporary,
All would be put right on the morrow,
In the meantime profess your total adoration
Of the loved one, what matter the missing hour,
Months, even years pass with no notice from you,
Not once did you hold your departed mother's entreating hand,
We have evidence suggesting you yourselves throttled the cuckoo bird,
What of value did you suppose yourselves to be doing today,
In any case?

21

We heard on the news from the very mouth of the utmost man who ought to know that we all are better off under him than any of us ever were before, which made us wonder how we and our pals somehow got excluded. 'If I ruled the entire world,' this monarch further said, 'the fullness of the universe would know no sorrow. Well, shucks, the stubbed toe, small scraps of sappy unhappiness now and again, let's say a flea bite, a wart springs up, I can't legislate removal of every quaint disorder, being human, you know, being humanistic, you might say. A fella says to me the other day, says, well, I forget now the exact words, something he'd heard on the broadcast news about the plague of astounding lies assailing his livelihood, what a crop of BS, I said to this crybaby, to hell with your warts, your bellyaches, when it comes to inundation of the seas, vain sea creatures taking affront, rest assured graver issues of that questionable magnitude ride high in my in-basket, my shined shoes are firm on the floor, your supreme commander is on the job.'

22

Time to call in the children for a confab. Sit down and be quiet, please. Understand, dear children, we are off to Zurich in the a.m. in a big leap for world peace, uniting of the Koreas, Cuban relief on the front-burner, flaming of remaining Nazi bunker high on the agenda, revitalization of world court a priority, restoration of looted antiques, reunion of lost sweethearts, elimination of ceaseless weeping whatever the cause. Unfortunately leaving your ears unwashed, broken goblets unswept from the floor, the rent unpaid, your stomachs unfed, grievous omission given that we take parenting seriously in this neighbourhood. Your schooling was, we trust, sufficient, your outlook adequate to the circumstances. Look for us not tomorrow or next week, what a relief to be shut of you always underfoot, phalanx of squealing rodents, accept that the Holy Ghostly Triad stands in awe of your sacrifices, your fine factory work the moment you ceased wetting your bed, that is if you had beds. Why, we have asked ourselves, coddle a child, who was there to coddle us, despite which it is your innocence, your welfare, we hold most dear. That's it, kids, the broken cup of mercy is obliterated, our best magicians have gone suicidal. Pardon, please, the dark moment, daylight is, you know, an illusion, full darkness beckons. To hell with it, to hell with everything, time to make entry into the Parlour of Inconsolable Gents and Maidens, to hell with them as well, when did you last ask yourself, why go on?

23

No, no, cried the fallen angel.
Why is she crying, we were asked.
Because they are beating her with sticks,
They are plucking her beautiful wings.
Why, we were asked. Because she was fallen, she had fallen
Headfirst into fraught society: these assailants
Did not like her looks, her disapproving air
Nor the very air whence she came.
She looked overfed to them. What
Justification those scabby knees,
The shucked toes,
'Gone grey from bad thoughts, I'd say.'
'Calls herself an angel, does she,
Try explaining that,
Who made her angelic in the first place?'

She wasn't a good angel, there are many bad ones, you know.
You only have to look around, turn your head, and there's another one
Pruning a rosebush, hanging clothes onto a line,
For freshness they will say.

Pay no attention to her sobs, this ladylike weeping,
Did Eve weep when baking her pie, her tears
Supplied the sweetness, this witch would say.
Odd that this lastest befallen, diminutive of figure
Brings to mind the chap Yakov Ivanov, maker of coffins, contemptuously
Denying measurement of boxes for departed children,
    declaring he couldn't abide
Troubling himself with trifles. Thus newborn and teen shuffled
    into identical conveyances
To other worlds.

OK, that's beside the point. Point is, not all the fallen are true angels.
I've witnessed fake angels falling daily by the hundreds.
I have in my backyard, in my attic, beneath my bed,
Scores of these creatures, mostly defrocked, pouting, wailing.

—Me too.

I watch them
At the dressing table brushing their hair,
Sitting opposite me at the breakfast table. I've determined
They can take any form, and often do at surprising moments,
Even sometimes as you are kissing them, wishing you could,
Or once did.

—Rings a bell.

This one they are today roughhousing is claiming innocence.
She has never claimed angelic kinship, how may her deeds
Be so misconstrued, how mysterious it is that anyone
        would suppose her
To be of that category. 'Why, heavens to Betsy, I was up all night
Looking after your crying baby.
Look, there is the very baby nodding assent. Assistance, please.

Feed this baby. Scotch this talk of fallen angels.
We must wash this child and ourselves. You do remember,
Do you not, dear husband, later today we are visiting
Your mother who has forgiven you
All your crimes save those
Applicable to me.'

24

Here lately have I been pondering
Who proposed to whom,
I to you or you to me or was it a third party
Lurching up from the grate unknown to either of us
But wanting his fifty cents.
How cavalier were we about money in those days
When we had none.
What were you wearing that day
When rack and ruin stood before us like an unfinished cathedral?
Was it night or day?
Did we have instant reply to those infamous summarizing words,
   Do you take ... ?

   (Recalled testimony:
   —You take your coffee black?
   —Si.
   —Why is that?
   —It did not require clairvoyance, my early youth, to know at times,
   for one in my line, refrigeration would be lacking.
   —Such foresight!
   Only that once.)

I am reasonably sure we were wearing nothing.
Surely all apparel had been stripped away.
Entire fortnights dressed in nothing!
Never such hunger, such speeches, such singing.
Rosy day take off into bliss.
Broadway (Sol Hurok Presents!) should have taken notice.

25

Must you mutter each time
We enter our bedroom,
Here goes nothing?
Was this something
An old girlfriend
Said to you?
I hear these deities'
Snickered delight
As I cover you
Or you me.
They wallow in with us,
A friendship thing,
I suppose.

26

We were stopped on the road by a troupe of dandelions asking
Could they sip mouthfuls of our water, please.
All in that polite nature they possess.
We have no water, we said, and were on the eve of asking you.
Then blow your sweet breath upon us, they said.
Tongue our tired roots into never-never land.
Bloat us with pasta alfredo followed by key lime pie.
Let us peruse your favourite magazines, comics, should you possess them,
Mutt & Jeff, that wolf fellow chasing the bird our favourites.
Then may it trouble you for us to pass the night on your chesterfield.
You will scarcely know we are here. We have
Business afoot come early morning wind and will off early.
Our annual convention is on the horizon, and know you are welcomed:
Ball games, taffy-pulling, log-rolling, horseshoes,
Nothing bacchanalian, be assured. It is difficult understanding the dislike,
The outright hatred you hold for us
Are we not pretty enough, more vigilant than sweet hyacinth,
Did we come over with uncouth Columbus, with unworshipping
    Polynesians before him
Oh, we thrived, but at what peril. We favour saying each night
    as we bed down, Our love
Is like a yellow, yellow dandelion, a schooled person
    will
    understand
    why.

27

The ghostly soul governing my body
Escapes through a latticed hatch,
Rising way out of reach.
Our dog, thinking this soul is his,
Pushes through the door
And winds down winding streets,
Shouting, You come back!

We each have scattered souls (elf-like) within the one,
Some yet unknown, as with biblical Eve's (she was discreet about it)
Thirty-three sons and twenty-three sons (Josephus said).
Poor Eve of moviedom possessed only three,
The identical number powered by this woman I love.
One is this minute hoisted upon a shelf trying to open
A can of peas, another cleans a befouled shoe.
The lazybones third (possibly the actual self) is just now waking up,
Wavering in the intention, moments ago, to hop into a bath
And remarking unto vacant air, *God save my breath,*
What an et tu Brute day yesterday was.

The returning dog deposits a bone beneath the author's knees.
Wuf-wuf, he goes, with pleading eyes. The author writing this poem
Recalls an Eric Fischl remark, not frivolously intended
Viz. *a painting oftentimes paints itself, will itself correct your mistakes.*
Will aggressively capture the brush from your trembling hand
And deftly apply radiant colour you never conceived.

Like when your beloved remarks that a better lover than you
Would have brought me flowers.
Which reminds me I'd best run out this minute
To Flower Central, inquire of the pretty attendant,
May I have a full bouquet like those Fischl gives his.

28

Hourly we
sling our word-waste into a barrel,
Sweet evening we bury this wastage ten meters
Into damp earth, kicking aside other barrels
Other poets left. See wide trails of trampled grass.
Come the day following this very page before you,
As with the bargained life,
Knows what to expect.

Why do you even bother rising from bed,
The grieving page complains. Soggy emptiness
Is all anyone ever expected of you.

You deserve it, breathes Beloved.
For not kissing me last night.

29

We were so excited when the sardine swimming
In olive oil escaped the tin
And more so to see the smart umbrella
Tilted above the sardine's head, less so
As we ate it with a dash of red pepper,
The umbrella reserved for tomorrow's rainy-day
stroll with friends.

30

The gnats circle in dizzying flight the spotted lamp
By the kitchen door. They are be-crazed by appetite
For my scalloped potatoes. If this experience is uncommon
To you the simple reason is my scalloped potatoes
Are more tasty than yours. You may ask my wife, out there
Swatting at gnats, the whole gang wanting to know is
That dish ready yet.

31

No valid stanza
Numbering 31
Adorns this page.
31 adjourned to another country
Where many dying poems go
To enjoy the ineffable splendour of laid-back repose.
31 was of discordant mind or it may be
Some floozie caught its eye.

32

The new piano was by the roadway weeping when an old man in a
donkey-cart picked her up. Too much Mozart's your trouble, the old
man said. Beside you there is my
    Sweetie Estrada dell Della
    Renowned songstress,
    Writes her own stuff.
Give this new piano a whiff of your goods, Della, dearest,
Cheer the sobbing sister up.
I don't normally perform for riffraff, Estrada dell Della said,
But then letting loose over gangbuster minutes a golden voice.
The new piano held her breath in wonderment
    at what she could never do,
Aware at once Mozart was not absolute antidote for every ill-deceit
The universe was heir to. I've been manic in my depression
Was the piano's purifying thought. How groovy the day
Was turning out to be.

Now Della was dive-bombing into the funky boozer tune 'Orphan's Lament,' the old man coming in steep on the melody, the new piano laying down a cool counter-rhythm as cloud-strewn day ambled into shimmering night.

❎

33

Today we were off to the ballpark,
The dastardly Muckrakers were in town,
Down ten by inning three, then beautiful rain.

Chess with the good lady tonight,
Kisses by the fireside,
Prelude to tomorrow when guests arrive,
Yourself among them though not invited.

34

The baby is adamant
She must herself have a baby to hold
If ever happiness is to be known.
They can share her crib, baby says,
And play with the stringed absurdity
In motion above her head—Calder's *Lobster Trap and Fish Tail*
Flung up on a day of heightened parental levity.
Baby wants the nursery
Overhauled before nightfall,
She believes it's time she learnt
Proper chewing: 'One of those freezer ribeyes
Will nicely accommodate my sighs,
Or am I to be dealt with as a freaked-out minion
Found on your doorstep?'

35

On that extra-rib question I figure some cranked-up old guy got on the horn, saying to some other wise-guy scripture guy, 'What do we say about this rib thing, take a look-see at Genesis 2:21, we way short of the goods in that patch,' this he's saying as he sees a runaway slave girl sprouting wings, in flight from his dungeon.

❌

36

The baby wants entertainment
In lieu of flattering words
Honouring her accomplishment.
Movies and popcorn she thinks
Will serve her needs.

37

We children, wayfarers under glow of sombre moons,
Scratchy product of happenstance, admit to confusion
In the family tree: how inventive parenting is these days,
All this talk of love depriving us of sleep, you'd think
We'd been belted within a bucking whirligig. All of us
Are not the breaking news, though some of us are,
Ask me not why. Daily do we wheel ourselves
To the Office of the Messenger of Truth,
There to be told we are to wait outside
On the painted bench beneath the dying elm.
Officers arrive in enforcement of this resolve
And by nightfall we find ourselves within a fenced enclave
Wherein stroll beasts of menacing intent
Which we are instructed not to harass
Else mayhem erupt, always an angry father shouting into my face,
Will this spoilt child of yours never sleep!

38

How wanton were these parents
To let the baby crawl out into the world
Naked and alone to scratch a path along
Cobbled pavement and scrabbled curb
Possibly in search of a saviour's inviting door.

She does well out there
Despite howling wolves, frost-sniffing wind,
Snow predicted for tomorrow,
Icefall the day after.

Back home, the chiggered baby
Plainly a maimed map of pain and sorrow,
No compliment proffered for
Her doleful eyes, her dappled chin,
The curled hair, the cupcake lips,
Pretty feet gone a demurring blue.

Just a lot of talk out there of baby fat,
Of public nudity hardly sacrosanct,
Of baby's short attention span,
Pundits' warning
Of the wasted life she will have.

39

The new piano was welcoming
Something triumphant is proposed
Rachmaninoff's Second,
Is our expectation.

40

When we fell in love
We were so irrational our feet hurt,
Deer tentatively tracking grass
To munch lovely leaves,
Robins scooting through wet.
We came upon a pond and swam
Through water cold as glass.
A moccasin wanting a taste
Trailed us numerous miles,
Our sticks whipping at snake
Gone bone-hopping mad,
Hissing as well:
What are your politics? asked running she,
Is *ethics* a word in your trousseau of forbidden words?
What emotion assails you when chanc'd upon a bird
Tumbled from nest? What frequency
The word *slipslop*
In Mr Joyce's *Ulysses*?
Frankly I find Descartes dull, do you not,
And Tolstoy's conduct unforgivable:
I quote, *Thither* did he seek peasants to rape.
At any rate all old news, however:
However, *in which room did what gender
Come and go*, what scribbler dispatched the echoing line
*Wanton troopers riding by
Have shot my fawn,
And it will die*?

Ultimately, my ultimate question implanted within
These many is what ultimate meaning you grant
To this life we may share.
Kindly speak not of bridges to be crossed
Please in the bargain to demonstrate you can be funny
Before, during, and after sex,
On what occasion is thievery justified,
If I confessed I left another man in tears,
Coming to you, would you consider mine a tawdry act?
I am desperately attracted but will it go to your head
No need for despondency,
One day you will better comprehend
The works of love
However foreign it be this current hour—
And would you kindly poke
That hooked-tooth pit viper cottonmouth from my heels,
Their bite can be deadly,
    of this
    you are aware,
    are you not?

    Such a crybaby!

41

A glass falls from the hand
Somersaults once
Landing on its own long stem
Not one droplet lost
This the goblet
To take home
The sweet cherry
Grinning there

42

Oh, bad day, huh,
So sorry to intrude.

43

Do not shoulder your bride aside
When she flashes off at the mouth
Accept your punishment for refusal
To eat your peas, know that sappy mother
Was up all night fending off blind sailors wanting beer
Wanting is a want has got me not far
Freedom is getting the falsetto notes right
Moon and sun experience customary seasons of disgust
Do we no longer celebrate my birthday in this house
And may I ask why
That elephant is sitting on you?

Dear luscious wife, in ages past I was
Dereliction-asleep on street grill
Windward to other freaks
Guarded over by vicious dogs,
Yet was so high of mind I was airborne,
I could venture through forest
With strength to strangle trees,
Now your sorry utterance has given boot
To every word.

Oh, heroic trees.
Drink this tea.

44

The pleasant woman
drinking champagne
from the glass
that earlier looped through air
losing not one drop
said it would be like beholding
in the doctor's famous poem
    those absurd chickens
    by the white wheel
    barrow,
at which point,
those within earshot
sought to hurl
the deluded
    critic
    over
    the grey
    fence

45

Friend Jim of Amherst
Has this poem: snowy day, pounding shore.
Comes along a youthful pair. The man
Drops his cloak at her feet, she lets fall hers to his.
Upon this bed they themselves lie down.
This is a work about sexual identity, the clothing industry,
Bad weather, superior home-schooling.
Will this coupling lead to full happiness?
Their destiny remains
    in your
    cool
    hands.
Bookies this minute are setting odds on you.

46

Those angels serenading us through
Hazardous night were rank songbirds chirping away
Mindless of hawks zooming overhead.
A new city ordinance decrees possible arrest, detention,
For our fake smiles

Like you're fleeing on foot from a robbed bank,
You've stuck up the dour employee

At We Cash Your Cheques, now your phony smile
At police officers blazing away.
The city believes you had this coming.
Is this not your city? Had you decamped
To Florida that day?

When you yesterday said
Today's sky would be blue
Were you thinking of me?

47

One thought was to take off my shoes
Only to discover them in another place.
Thought I'd go to bed, instead discovered I already was there
Together with another party lost in Elsewhere.
I was in mind of your blue eyes coming through the door
Of your blue blouse abandoned to floor
Holding you, I had thought
Of land for sale in Peru,
The non-Peruvian you
explored.

48

A fine poem
Said Edward John
Trelawny
Of this one
After lifting
Percy Bysshe's heart
From the fire and running home
With the heart smoking.
Inside the valise
Borrowed from
Byron who had
Been found sitting beneath
A drooping willow
Smiling
Into the grey beyond

49

We call
and call
the cat
and the cat's eyes
shift our way
as it continues
to crouch
in the rain

50

Crisis Management Report—We got the smut wiped up in record time.
We love our work—the shoeshine parlour, the dog wash,
    upkeep of church bathrooms.
Summer camp wasn't that glorious, though.

Soak the woman's feet in brine.
Chafe the elbows.
Plait the hair before she's off
To work the cane field.

51

While alive Emily published in Amherst
Five poems.
Death came and some seventeen hundred and more
Were discovered neatly bundled
In her bedroom desk.
For fifteen years she never left
The family home.
Some say at night's darkest hour
She emerged to water grass.
That may be true.
I believe at night in her long white dress
She pole-vaulted. She traipsed, she ran.

52

Hello, darling, here's tea. Was yours a very nice day?

Why, Cassandra, how sweet of you to ask. This very day
I wrote in mellow verse form a story about ourselves,
called 'Rank Songbirds.' Every word not finding its way to the page
I swear to be utter truth. I believe I shall have wine.

53

Good morning.
Repeat after me:
In the beginning of time
Was nothing but soup,
You couldn't walk upright,
You couldn't stoop,
Was no heaven,
Was no hell,
Black moon ruled
The black moonlight,
You had no speech,
You had no sight.

Now, please, to get yourself dressed,
Carry trash to curb,
Kiss your baby,
Kiss the wife,
Mouth the mariner's pledge
(No more drink).

Songbird Sonatarina

ONE, she called him on the phone, she said, Where have you been? he said, Here, here, all day I've been here, she said, Hours I've been calling you, he said, I doubt that, what do you want? she replied in a particularly heightened, some would say piqued voice, as if struck by a seizure of some kind, *What do I want?* he said, Only six in the evening and already you've gone haywire, she said, I have not, in fact, I'm coming over, I'm on my way, I have in fact arrived, in another minute I'm coming through your door, he said, Try not to mow down that nice magnolia I today planted by the driveway, I see it, she said, that's dogwood not magnolia, he said I hope you've brought dinner—but didn't think she heard that part because what he heard was the close-by slamming of a car door. This is the way they talk, let's try to accustom ourselves to the peculiar, not everyone in the world is as wonderful as we are.

TWO, her car door, that lousy teensy muzzle-shot bumper-dragging Pinto heap she thought she looked so hot in.

THREE, this was in the spring, in the spring of the year this was, at his house by the river, oh not so distant from the river one couldn't see it, a fact which was far from the case during the last rainy season when the river slurped right up to the door she was about to enter, in fact, although it wouldn't occur to her on this visit, she had stored in uneasy memory a time when the river made entry into the very bedroom she did not expect today, for a wide variety of reasons, to set one foot into, one of those select reasons being today he had been huffy with her, his prissy voice when answering the phone, that bizarre accusation, my goodness, she thought, passing through the door, that door desperately needing a paint job, a woman can take but so much, plus what cause has he to be thinking my duty is to hustle in his dinner, a good dinner doesn't come cheap, and would he ever think to reimburse me, not in this lifetime. Cheap, I'm not about to tolerate cheapness in a man I don't like that much in the first place, no matter how handsome he is, smooth as a jackal, some other woman might say, not me, thank you, Teddy Roosevelt.

FOUR, for his part, he damned well did remember it, the river washing through, the bed wallowing about in aimless floatation, her full naked self exclaiming, *This is no way to entertain a woman,* am I a Seabee, you think, oh, my foot just fell in. Not that the Seabee mention has any relevance at the moment, exercise patience, the Seabee stuff comes later.

FIVE, he ventured, not very deftly, onto a favoured subject while they were eating hot dogs discovered in the fridge, on bread slices gone stale, Everybody curses this man you're so hot on, God and the devil alike curse him, everybody who knows him curses him. What she said, with an abruptness always startling to him, was *I love him.* Three times she said this, as was her habitual custom, *I love him, I love him, I love him,* so utterly composed in this recitation he thought it almost inconceivable, there they are eating these past-the-consumption-date hot dogs when he's reasonably certain they are soon going to be in the bedroom kissing each other as lovingly as they know how, or at least kissing the way each can be certain the parties like well enough to keep on kissing. Not that this soon-to-be kissing stopped him from pressing on with his report of the massive congregation of humanity which ceaselessly cursed this man she purportedly was so hot on. He said, His mother curses him, his father does, brothers and sisters cry foul at your lover guy's presence, not one party to my knowledge has ever muttered one good word about him, no, they curse him to the ends of the earth, I for one curse the very earth he walks upon. She responded, in her usual foggy state when so challenged, with her customary *I love him, I love him, I love him. They don't know him the way I do,* by rote saying this, as if truly befogged, as though this love was close to being a religion with her, as though she was lip-syncing a tuneless rune sent her from an alien star. And this same she was saying as the sun was casting its final shadow, and she went on repeating *I love him,* into full darkness she did, as he busily set forth the very names and occupations of those cursing this presumed lover, adding the whys and wherefores, vile incidents giving rise to these curses, she then adding, *It's true I often cursed him myself, though I loved and love him, and ever shall.* Yeah, he said, well, I call this a sad-sack-type of love, a guttersnipe-type love, it's puppy-love in adult neurotic disguise, it's love akin to that type of love a monarch reputedly has for those said to be the monarch's subjects, which we both know is a bogus, fabricated deal designed to keep society's engine oiled. She quivered at that statement, her shoulders shot straight back, her eyes shrouded, her fists clenched, she said, That's socialist talk, you sound exactly like my friend Ringo the socialist when you talk like that, I like the idea of kings and queens, especially I like the princess-and-prince part, everybody does except you and my friend Ringo the socialist. His shoulders shot back, he said, Who is this Ringo hotshot you keep mentioning, maybe he's another guy you can't help drooling over, I'd like one day to meet both these gooney-birds you got the hots for, I'd like to give them a royal punch in the snout. Ha, she said, they'd each beat you up, you'd be horsemeat, them two are bulldogs. *Them two?* It's true what her parents claim, she likes giving the impression she's less smart than these parents think she is.

SIX, here she coughed three times, she vacated the bed she'd found unmade, it always was a bed unmade, such a sloppy housekeeper, he probably was one of those loonies believing any household task was a woman's work, men laid bricks, they threw plaster on walls, they planted a dogwood sapling they called a magnolia tree, the female did everything else. This so enraged her sometimes she had coughing fits.

SEVEN, here was the day they were on the road, in his car driving somewhere, anywhere, no specific goal in mind, he was remembering on a recent journey her lavish exclamation on the order of *Watch Out! Watch Out!*, watch out for that big boulder on the road, for that burnt car on the shoulder, look, there went a drunk driver, somebody better watch out, I don't know why people can't just slow down, everybody in a hurry to get nowhere they must get to, on and on she went in that shaky, peril-awaits-us voice so mysteriously received by the attending nerves, her feet pressing, those hands waving, I've the funny feeling this road empties into a suicidal cliff people leap from, these ill-bodings that time proving meritorious, however, because scant miles further on they'd arrived at a barrier in the road, numerous law people swooping upon them, what's going on, officer, he said, get slowly from the car, one of these said, hands in the air, no sudden moves. You mean just him, she said, or us both? All the officers taking a long look at her, one finally saying, No, little lady, you just sit tight, keep those legs crossed.

EIGHT, it was also on that journey, the Pinto pulled into a roadside hideaway, the day getting on towards dark, that she said, No, I won't marry you, but that doesn't mean you must stop kissing me. A short while later, she said, Now where did I put those shoes, I am reasonably certain I was wearing shoes, he said, Now hold on, I never precisely asked you to marry me, mine was a statement merely swimming around the subject, kind of like you're fishing, you spot a big one, but before you get your hook on the line that fish has shot off some other place, she said, It's hard to believe my shoes could have plumb disappeared, he said, Some other guy gets that fish.

NINE, ... pursuant to our earlier discussion, two clichés of paramount significance in my homelife, my growing years, I neglected to mention, one, *I Wasn't Born Yesterday*, two, *I Knew You When*, Mother has always wanted both on her headstone, one to either side. *Sop to Cerberus* my father, his eminence, his lordship, avers is of formidable enterprise when beset by the riffraff encircling his court, shall I go on?

TEN, 'Listen to me,' she said.
'I'm done listening,' he said. 'I've wiped the slate clean, I've purged from memory every word you ever said.'
'What about last night?' she said. 'What I said after what you said?'
'There was no last night. Last night went over the cliff.'
'You went over the cliff, I found a haven in the ceaseless flow of tears. Tears you disparaged because that's the kind of rat-fink you are.'
'You've cracked up, you know. That's the kind of woman you are.'
'Not true. I've won awards—from the YWCA, for instance—for my show of common sense midst disturbing circumstances, overwhelming obstacles, absolutely terrifying ordeals.'
'Like a fingernail broke. You saw a loose end.'
'More like the person you love best in the world drops dead right in front of you, say like on the most beautiful summer day your eyes have ever been a part of.... At summer camp I won the leadership badge three years running, I led us all in the evening prayer, all those things I had to make up that we could be thankful for.'
'That's nothing to boast of.'

'What award did you ever win except Heel of the Year?'
'I'm not listening.'
'You were happy to listen last night when my arms were around you.'
'Last night was another country. That country went over the cliff.'
'Are you going to make us breakfast?'
'Don't I always? When did you ...'
'I'll go and get dressed.'
'No, you won't, I only serve breakfast to naked women whose stomachs are so flat one may shoot marbles on them, and are often asked to, that's the type of belly my women have.'

ELEVEN, he said. I want to tell you—she interrupted. I'd rather you didn't, he said. The kind of story that keeps my nose to the page, like the book I'm reading now, or was until you stomped through the door, is the story that starts nowhere, goes nowhere, and you never are introduced to the main character, the character I mean who is supposed to promote and propel the narrative, I find stories of that sort deeply fulfilling, these tales rattle around in my gut and make me think life is truly worthwhile. She said, You slap plaster on walls, you dig ditches, you're a low-caste handyman, what do you know? He was undeterred, he said, The people I like best, for instance, my entire family, are those who are dumber than tree stumps, I mean the kind who never learn to tie a shoelace, these are the heroic types I most admire, the diligence required of them in an environment reviling them, don't imagine these poor saps lack perception of their plight, those are our true heroes, and that's been the case throughout history, those of my ilk get cut down with the same ease your father cuts his grass.... Are you done? she asked, my father doesn't cut grass, he hires crybaby people like you to do it, my favourite heroes, other than Ringo the socialist, are those who shimmy down a post to hurry off and put out a fire. Also, she said, I stand to correct you, new science informs us that tree stumps, trees, generally, are anything but dumb, trees form a universe unto themselves, I include mere bushes in this, wild blackberry vines I list as prime example of artful intelligence shared among bushes, a living tree is of kindred spirit with other trees, it aids brother and sister trees when in distress, moreover, a tree you've cut down, your begrudged stump, goes on desperately and unseen extending its living roots, my very father poured ten gallons of poison on a tree he cut down, he blasted that stump right and left, and the next spring there were dozens of vigorous saplings saying hello. Okay, I stand corrected, he said, I don't claim to know everything, in fact what I do know, know with assurance, wouldn't fill a pint bucket, what I think happens is that when I sleep all knowledge drains out of me in my sweat and my jerky movements and my endlessly reaching for you, only to find you've gazoomed off to some other place, I wake howling my misery, where did she go, why did she leave me, why doesn't she remain one minute where she last was? She said, I'll tell you why, I love him, that's why, you I hardly even know, you're the kind my mother warned me about, well, truthfully, what Mother said is, I quote verbatim, Try to avoid the kind of man your father proved to be, and I don't mean to suggest your father isn't decent and kind in his own way, but but but. She went on with these buts through dinner, through endless night, and at breakfast she had a whole new handful of these buts, my God, such a mouth that woman my mother has, if I chanced to see her this minute I bet she's still rattling off these buts, while at the same time if I say *I'm so sorry darling mother you're locked within an unhappy marriage* she'll take the roof off hollering, What are you talking about, I'm the happiest woman alive, I wouldn't change your dear father for the crown prince of Arabia, not for the gold mines of Sultana would I swap him, why, do you wish to know why, because he IS the crown prince of Arabia and if you were not such a selfish prig and dog in a blanket and had as much as a toe in the real world you would know that, etc., etc., see what I mean?

TWELVE, do you? Do you see what I mean? ... Wait, wait, where did he go?

THIRTEEN, where did he go, why is he doing this to me?

FOURTEEN, such a rotter, rotter, rotter, rotter, excuse me if I pour myself a drink.

FIFTEEN, officer, officer, be kind, I promise you it was only one drink, possibly two.

SIXTEEN, Daddy, Daddy, this ruffian policeman wants to cart my butt off to Sing Sing, Daddy, he's being so horrid, so I was weaving on the road a teensy bit, I've always had trouble with that Pinto's steering, Daddy oh Daddy, you sit on the bench, a big-time judge like you are, you tell this twerp what for, rake his guts, my God, one little drinkie!

SEVENTEEN, precious, precious, thank you, Daddy. Yes, officer, I do apologize, I don't know what compelled me to say those awful things to you, sir, I hold the forces you represent in the highest utter regard, I've often thought I missed a turn by not, not entering the law-force-field—What? What, what, what, I looked so sexy trying to walk that line, what, you want to kiss me? …

EIGHTEEN, some items we've neglected to properly report, for instance when she made that insulting remark about his plastering business, that brick-laying stuff, he got on his high horse about that, he was as they say fit to be tied, in no uncertain terms did he tell her, Say what you like about my humble employment, browbeat the lowly working man, the besieged labourer who at minimum wage daily walks the plank into oblivion, but you overlook what's important here, like what's important here is who, who or what, a technically proficient craftsman such as yours truly is capable of, like at any time, should I decide to, I can seal away with those bricks, with that plaster, anyone getting my goat, like for instance you if you again go high-hat cutesy on me, I read Poe in high school, you know. You know?
    What, what what! You want to seal me away?
    Yeah, and what else is this Seebee thing you mentioned, I never heard the word Seebee, Seebiscuit, now, Seebiscuit was a racehorse of amazing speed, acumen, and dexterity, but Seebee's got me beat.
    She said, after a time:
    Can you hear this woman speaking to you from her sealed compound?
    I hear you.
    I'll have you know the Seabees are an illustrious outfit attached to the navy, my father the illustrious judge was a Seabee serving in Chi Mai, no, Chi something, during the Vietnam war, they are into construction and such, I should think a famous plaster Cask

of Amontillado genius like you would know that. Yes, he said, well, I didn't know, like what else I didn't know was when I planted my pretty magnolia by my driveway I'd somehow drifted over into old Mrs. Wadmore's property, there she is knocking on my door telling me where I can git off, because in the addition I've slung in that magnolia on the very spot where she long ago buried her dead cat Fluffie. He was interrupted, freed now from her self-imposed vault she said, Yeah, well, that was not the way I heard that story.

NINETEEN, how I heard that story is that he and that strung-out old mophead Wadmore have been in warfare the whole of their lives, but listen, Ringo, are you tuned in, that ratty old dame today said to my face you show too much bosom, she said, I wouldn't be caught dead in skirts up to my crotch, she said, but that wasn't all, next she said even at her age her legs were better than mine, this was after we'd had a spat about the kind of tree it was. What tree, asked Ringo the socialist, but at that moment she heard a sudden thud or bang, and Ringo saying, Got to go, somebody just shot at me, Mr Kissinger and his gang must be in town.

TWENTY, sorry, I can't talk to you now, I've got to slap plaster on this wall, this is a twenty-dollar-an-hour job and I'm telling you they don't come my way every day, where are you, if you're with that lusty bastard everybody curses, then I'm not talking to you ever again. Sez you, sez you, she says back, it's none of your business who I'm with or not with, so put that in your pipe and smoke it, Godamighty, he comes back, almost apoplectic in her view, I never met a mortal so quick to leap from the diving board with another excruciating cliché, I have heretofore viewed you as an educated woman, goodbye. Quick on the draw, she lets fly with, Anybody frothing at the mouth from a person's use of a time-honoured cliché is a dumb-bunny twenty-dollar-an-hour horse's ass whose very brain has become a bowl of fruit jelly, mouldy plaster in your case, you are obviously not *au fait* to the current and developing movement seeking to restore the cliché to its rightful place at the head of the societal beehive, I need mention that only yesterday his eminence the pope said, and I quote, *In our soaring into heaven we go as the crow flies*, the hottest band on the planet this minute is

In a Pig's Eye the hotshot motion picture Academy Award nominees are for you, only to find you've gazoomed off to some other place, I wake howling *Tale Between the Legs* and *Happy as a Clam, I Shed Krokodile Tears* is the banner title in the book race, he said, That's a bunch of bull you are making up, she rose to her tippy toes, saying, I'm expecting you to be at my door by seven o'clock tonight, bring dinner, I'll try my best to be home.

TWENTY-ONE, ego, ego, both seem jacked up with this high opinion of themselves. So, all right, her father (*Daddy, Daddy, Daddy!*) is a judge, the mother comes from, and has, money, his father a dishwasher, his mother a grade-school dropout, nothing shameful in those pursuits, the time they first met she was wearing a short high-above-the-knee suede skirt, crotch-level you might say, those legs startling to gaze upon, the skirt a juggernaut to get past, he didn't exactly praise her for this smashing dress debut, because in those days he didn't talk much, just that smouldering expression on his face, rabid opinion reserved for the brighter day, he's a dope, classmates said, he didn't impress me either was her private testimony, uncanny how he can be confused with so many others, she had been heard to say, it was like I was beholding a brigade of prize twerps, it's like I'm living with, mooching with, bedding with, dining twice weekly with … with a … a … you know what I was about to say. This the two of them were taking turns recounting to Ringo the socialist, a swell guy who was turning out to be his best buddy, he wondered now how he'd ever come up with the suspicion Ringo the socialist had been a competitor in the love sweepstakes, a number-one staunch guy of the first rank was Ringo the socialist, they were extraordinarily happy to hide Ringo away from Mr Kissinger and his anti-socialist anti-commie anti-everything-but-us goons, they took heart from Ringo's every word, from Ringo who now had the floor and was saying we are all siblings of the lost years surrounded by depression-era fundamentalists looping into religious fervour in the vain hope, the deluded expectation of continued racism, exhortation of … and so forth and so forth, Ringo said, a blabbermouth Mr Kissinger would call him, all these so-called high-assed progressives are.

TWENTY-TWO, don't be silly, she earlier, much earlier, had told him,

Ringo's special, I love Ringo, but I have no feelings for him the way you are talking about, don't be a jealous nutcake, Ringo's so hung up on what was done to Cuba, to Chile, El Salvador, those countries, that he can be a pill to be around, my father his judgeship agrees it was that dope-runner Secretary of State Kissinger largely to blame, him being the brainy one, no way he can be forgiven for combatting insurrections, for igniting wars, for having got Allende killed.... Ah, so here today this pair is, first hour of a long weekend, feeling refreshed after a long sleep deep and true, working hours a big pile behind them, Ringo the socialist stashed away at his firebrand sister's, the highway stretching in sunlit splendour before them, traffic a shade too crowded for comfort but nothing to lose steam over.

Oh
it's so marvellous, said she, to relieve oneself of the humdrum, to breathe the fresh air, to have a whole day devoted to naught but irregularity, I'm so happy I could sing, I think I shall. And by God, she did, what a voice was his divine thought, pure as that Brit girl Sandy Denny, who wrote and performed at age twenty that monumentally fantastic song 'Who Knows Where the Time Goes,' a version sustained impeccably by another top-flight Brit, Eva Cassidy, then along comes Nina Simone in whispers to knock that song out of the ballpark, what I listen to, he said, had been repeatedly saying, when slapping on the plaster, but here my girl is possessing talent heretofore unknown, up there with those very star-busters, and in her own style too, dynamite, heck, I didn't know she could carry a tune but here improvising the lyrics as her cherubic voice challenges the scales, roping in the highs and lows, his a sturdy hand-beat on the Pinto's fragile dash, a perfect moment was the secret thought of each, by God I've got to marry this plum, and if anybody here believes this is when the tire blows and the Pinto soars over the cliff and they die a terrifying death then the author doesn't want to know you, this is destined to be a happy story, whatever else you may have hoped for.

TWENTY-THREE, so you're the cad my daughter has been seeing were the first words from the judge's lips on the day she took him *home to dinner with the flashbacks*, words he received sombrely, Mother holding herself stiffly in the far regions, hawkeyes upon him, there not being the smallest glimpse of dinner anywhere on the horizon, a ruse of mine, she said later, *In the event we had to make a fast escape*, which they did fast make, neither parent in a mood for prolonged palaver once they had caught sight of you, she said, their noses turned high as if both were thinking *Is that the best she can do*, that has ever been their attitude, she said, about any boy I ever brought home, it's a vanity number they play, his being an eminence and all, most of the time they are nice and noble and soft as sorghum molasses, whereas he took issue with her description of the parental welcome, saying, with what she thought of as a sickening smile on his face, It was clear his eminence and your mother liked me, both were all ears in respect to my dogginess in the building trade, they both said my presence in your life was making a new girl out of you, in high flight one day, elegiac the next, a flush in your cheeks you never had before, affable as a rogue cat, yes, your daddy said, *Clearly as a pipe dream you two will perform quite the pas de deux*, lovely, huh? They had on the coffee table any number of bowls filled with different nuts we could eat, your pop for your birthday wants to shuffle this Pinto into the graveyard, gift you a BMW, your mom offered to lend me money for a new suit, Papa took his tie off and draped it round my neck, wasn't that thoughtful of them? Oh, she said, I didn't see that, I must have been choking on my tea biscuit or up checking out my old room, it's Mother's hideaway now, what a hoot, would you ever guess she collects baby doll antiques? What's more, he quickly said, is both confirmed to me you've been half loco, had that imagined lover pal in your life, since that time before you were housebroken, sitting on your dad's knee watching that Jim Stewart movie about the guy with the rabbit.

TWENTY-FOUR, but which place would we live, said she, mine is nicer, closer to town, the amenities, you might say, whereas yours is roomier, you have the more resplendent view. Resplendent, huh, he said, she said, There's that muddy river one can see from your place, at least from your rooftop or climbing a tree we'd have that river to look at when we had nothing else to do. And the money we'd save, he said, on gas, all that running back and forth your place to mine, the wear and tear, a guy can git old doing that. She said, Ha, I didn't know seeing me brought on such ache and pain. I didn't say that, he said, but Christ, the number of speeding tickets I've got rushing over to your place. She said, What tickets, what are you talking about, heckfire, he said, I'd git the jitters just thinking about seeing you. Me too, she said, the pounds would shake right off me. But here's something to think about, she said, it can't be said we get along together that well, your politics are way goofier than mine, you often turn wild hog over nothing at all. Now you just wait a minute, he said, you know you've got a big mouth that runs off at full gallop especially on nights when the moon is full, I do not, she said, he said, As an example of your shallowness, your conceit, your thoughtlessness, you kept harping about that door, a thousand times you told me to paint that door—*Paint the door, paint the door!* you kept screaming—I painted that door, gave it a cheerful blue, nice as a sacrificial lamb that door now is, yet have you said one word about it, not one, likely you haven't even noticed I painted the damn door. She said, Oh I noticed it all right, my first thought was that blue was the drabbest blue anyone ever set eyes on, no one would describe that blue as a captivating Van Gogh blue, you need to redo that door in something like a forest green, yes, a forest green to match that pathetic tree the grouchy old lady made you pull up, plus you had put that tree in the very spot where she had buried her old cat Fluffie, Fluffie wasn't going to like that, or whatever she said Fluffie's name was. By the way, she went on, you got your facts twisted on that singer girl you get hot flashes thinking about, that Eva party, she was American-born though the Brits put her in the limelight, I've rapidly come to the conclusion one may not believe a word you say. To this he said, Listen to you, he said, just listen, I can't be expected to know every little detail about a person's life, heckfire, what do we know about our own, for that matter, or what's coming next?

TWENTY-FIVE, he then said, Well, let's do it anyway, what's the harm, we don't stand a chance in hell but it doesn't work I'll just throw you out in the rain the way I would any other scrap-assed thing, You think so, huh, she said, I'm clear on what midget-brain will get thrown out, but all right let's give it the old heave-ho, sally forth with the best intent, come old age we will be two bent wrecks washed up on the tide of ineptitude, it's well-known *I give full support to any lost cause.*

TWENTY-SIX, Don't you? Don't you?

Acknowledgements

Ace poets George Bowering, Roger Greenwald, Edward Carson, and scholar/critic Samuel Solecki read, possibly with misgivings, an early draft, offering useful suggestions (GB: 'Mind those lame line endings'; RG: 'Suggest you set sections nearer to prose than poem in prose format'; SS: 'Change Beethoven to ... Alter sequence ... End with ...' EC: 'More mythical Greek goddesses ... these, for instance ...' Did I listen? You bet. Poet Derk Wynand, long-time friend, presumably in rushed reading, said: 'I give it four stars ... Friend I passed pages on to gave it five.' Notice to readers—Blame them for this book.

Otherwise. The hallowed, flawless gang at Porcupine's Quill ('40-plus years on Main Street!') are owed the author's praise and gratitude: Tim and Elke Inkster, spirited proprietors, Chandra Wohleber, impassioned editor ('A bad line drops me dead to the floor'), Stephanie Small, ever crucial to the enterprise and Keeper of the Tides ('I promised myself certain promises as a young child and my intent is to remain true to these RULES PERTAINING TO LIFE, however jeopardizing'). Thanks, all.